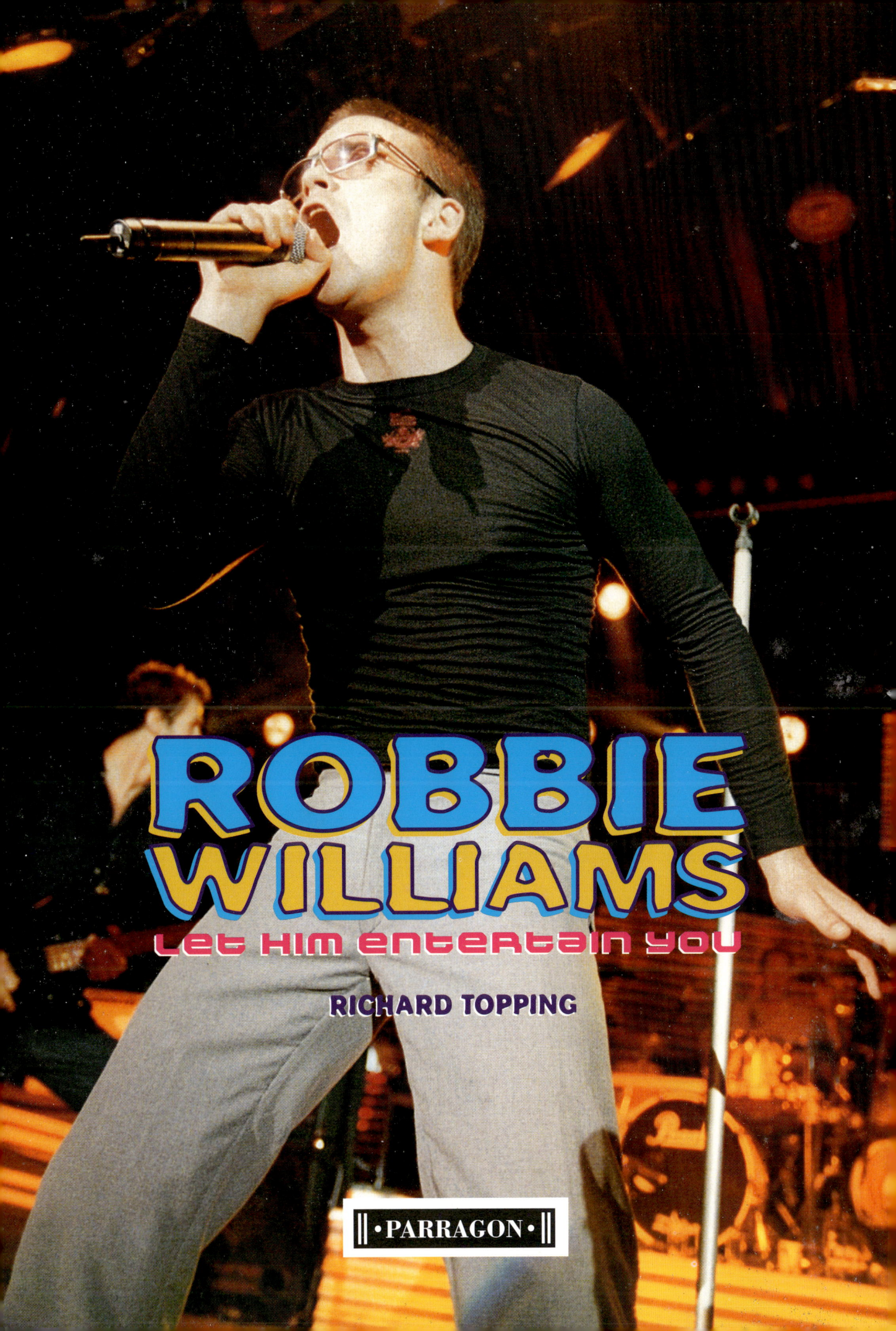

# ROBBIE WILLIAMS
Let Him Entertain You

RICHARD TOPPING

|| •PARRAGON• ||

First published in 1999 by
Parragon
Queen Street House
4 Queen Street
Bath
BA1 1HE

Copyright © 1999 Parragon

Produced by Blackjacks

All rights reserved. No part of this publication may be reproduced, stored in a retrieval system, or transmitted by any means, electronic, mechanical, photocopying, recording or otherwise, without the prior permission of the copyright holder.

British Library Cataloguing-in-Publication Data

A catalogue record for this book is available from the British Library.

ISBN 0 7525 3246 4

Printed in Italy

Contents

I've Been Expecting You	4
No Regrets	6
Phoenix From The Flames	8
Let Me Entertain You	10
Ego A Go Go	12
She's The One	14
Life Thru A Lens	16
Man Machine	18
Heaven From Here	20
One Of God's Better People	22
Win Some, Lose Some	24
Millennium Man	26
The Brits	28
These Dreams	30

i've been expecting you

There's no getting away from it – Robbie Williams is the undisputed king of pop. Once the bad boy in top band Take That, Robbie has reinvented himself as everyone's favourite pop star. He's been nominated for more Brit awards than anyone in the history of pop music, his first album's gone double platinum and his second is catching up fast. He's a joker, an entertainer, a songwriter, a singer, a dancer and all-round nice bloke. And if his career keeps going the way it's started, it looks like he'll end up being the biggest music star ever!

But the road to becoming pop's main man hasn't always been paved with good times. There's been plenty of tears along the way as well. His story – from self-confessed 'useless' double glazing salesman thru pop pin up to solo megastar – shows there's more to Robbie than grins and great tunes.

Robert Peter Williams had a fairly normal childhood. His mum Theresa and comedian dad Pete Conway ran a pub called the Red Lion next to Port Vale's football ground. When he was three, Robbie's parents split up and he, his mum and his sister Sally went to live on an estate in Stoke.

Robbie took after his dad, always playing the clown in class. He loved being the centre of attention, and after joining a local theatre company landed a few parts in musicals like *Fiddler On The Roof* and *Oliver*. He even got himself a tiny part in TV soap *Brookside*.

After leaving school and trying to sell double glazing, Robbie decided he wanted to be a professional actor. But poor old Robbie went to every audition he could find without getting a single part! Then his Mum saw an advert for a four man band that wanted a fifth member, and she persuaded him to audition. The band was called Take That, and Robbie had taken the first step to mega-pop stardom!

"I'm an actor who somehow found himself in the music business," says Robbie. "I want to be a musician but I also want to be an actor."

No Regrets

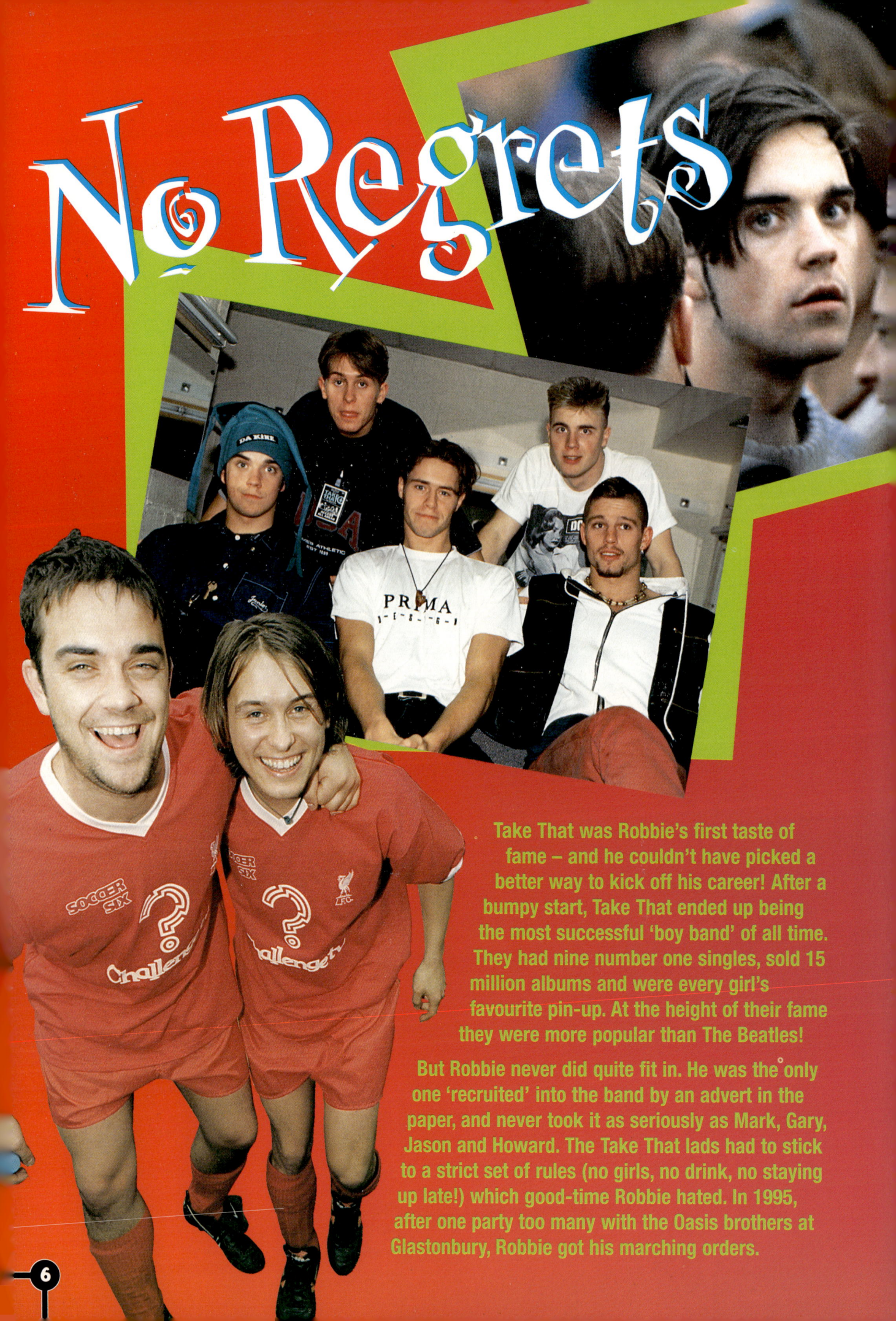

Take That was Robbie's first taste of fame – and he couldn't have picked a better way to kick off his career! After a bumpy start, Take That ended up being the most successful 'boy band' of all time. They had nine number one singles, sold 15 million albums and were every girl's favourite pin-up. At the height of their fame they were more popular than The Beatles!

But Robbie never did quite fit in. He was the only one 'recruited' into the band by an advert in the paper, and never took it as seriously as Mark, Gary, Jason and Howard. The Take That lads had to stick to a strict set of rules (no girls, no drink, no staying up late!) which good-time Robbie hated. In 1995, after one party too many with the Oasis brothers at Glastonbury, Robbie got his marching orders.

When Take That split up a few months later, it was Gary Barlow who was supposed to go onto big solo success. But things worked out differently. It turned out Robbie - the clown prince of Take That who no-one took seriously - was the real star in the making.

"If you're gonna be in a boy band, be the best in the world," says Robbie. "And I'm really proud to say that I was in the best of the bunch!"

PHOENIX FROM THE FLAMES

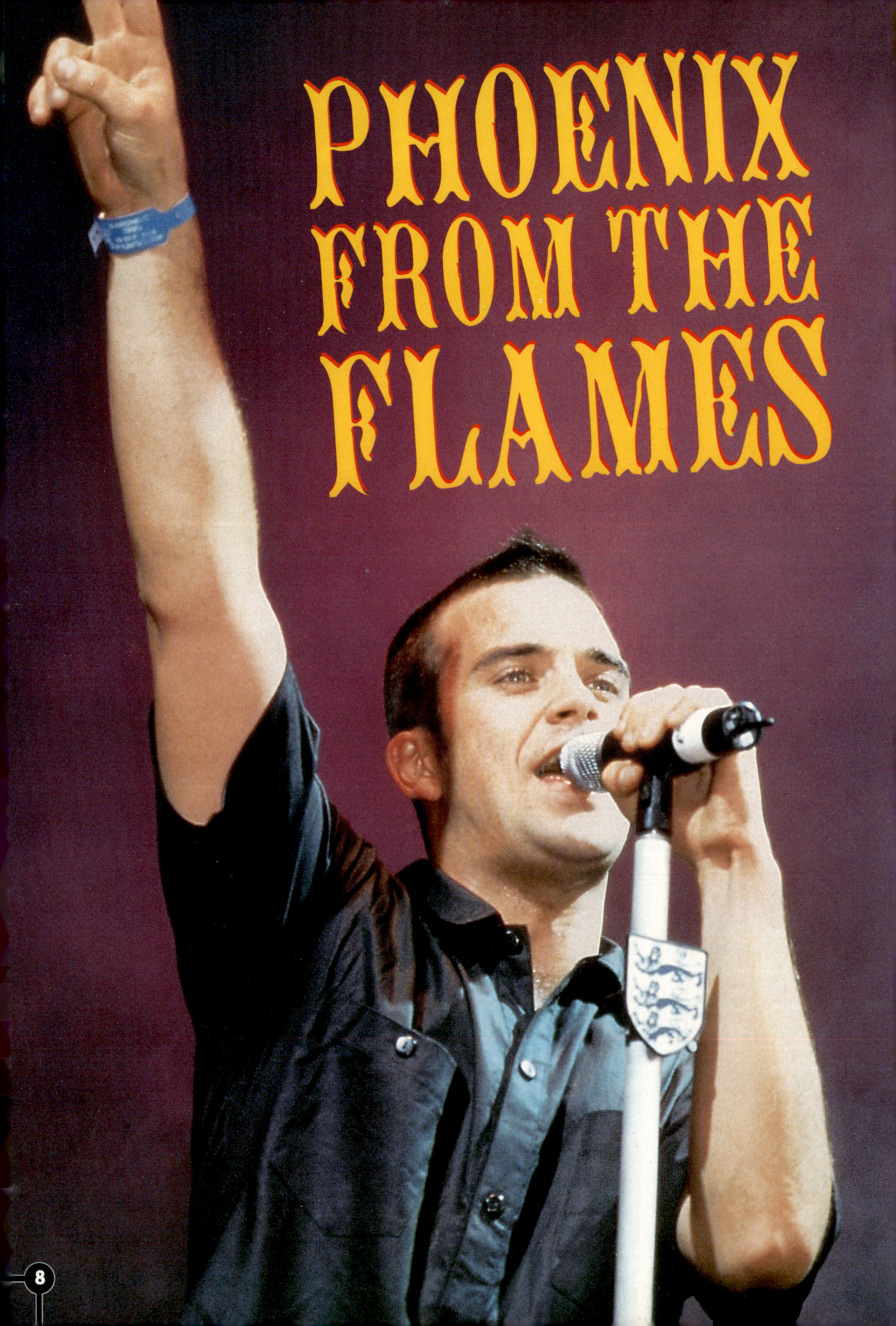

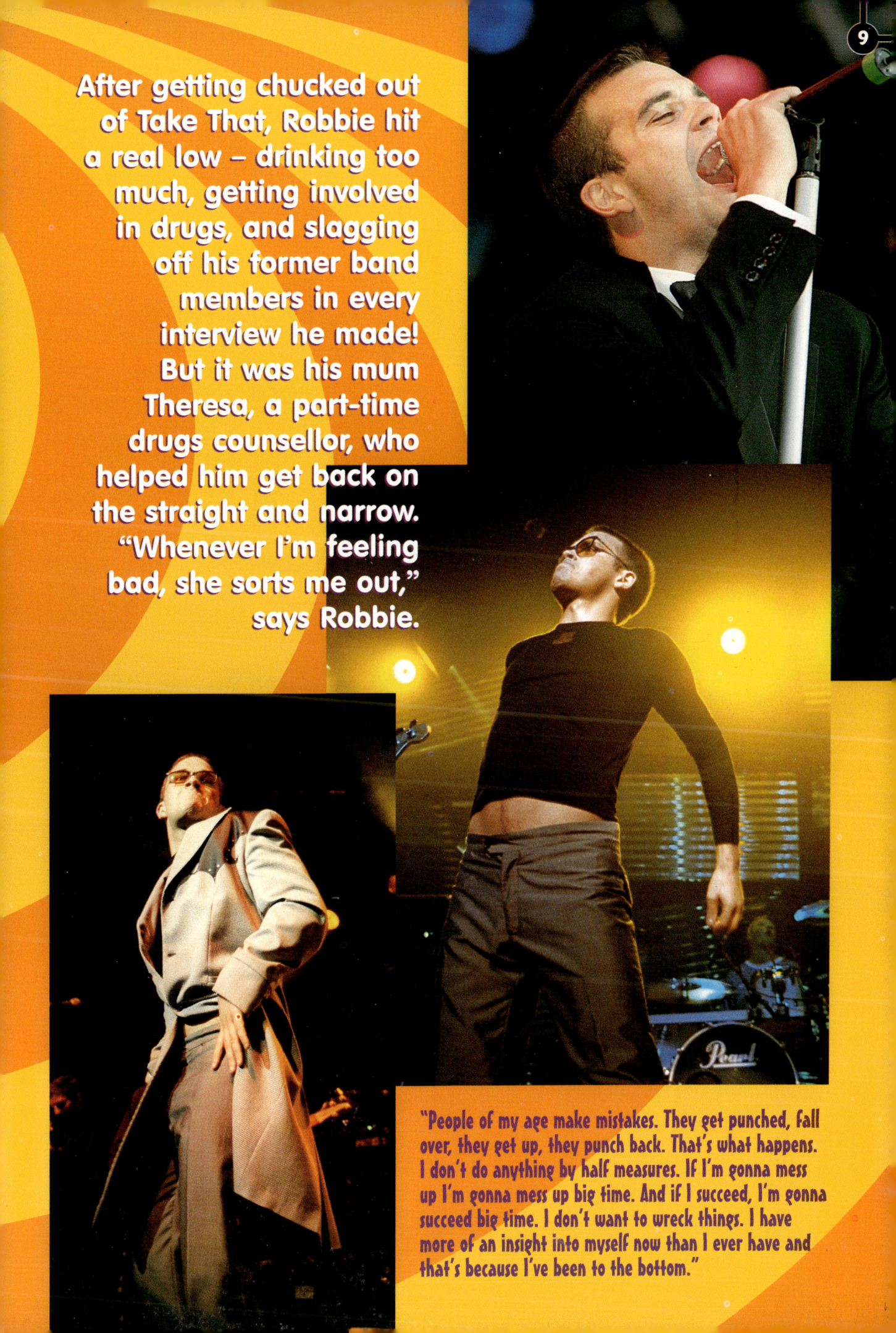

After getting chucked out of Take That, Robbie hit a real low – drinking too much, getting involved in drugs, and slagging off his former band members in every interview he made! But it was his mum Theresa, a part-time drugs counsellor, who helped him get back on the straight and narrow. "Whenever I'm feeling bad, she sorts me out," says Robbie.

"People of my age make mistakes. They get punched, fall over, they get up, they punch back. That's what happens. I don't do anything by half measures. If I'm gonna mess up I'm gonna mess up big time. And if I succeed, I'm gonna succeed big time. I don't want to wreck things. I have more of an insight into myself now than I ever have and that's because I've been to the bottom."

Robbie's a self-confessed show-off, and loves nothing more than being on stage in front of an audience! He's got his own five man band and even plays the guitar himself. He comes alive when he's playing to a crowd and has so much energy even the band can't keep up with him sometimes!

"I'm a born entertainer," says Robbie "When I open the fridge door and the light comes on, I burst into song. Up on stage, I do whatever I want – no dance routines, nothing. I forget all about my troubles for a couple of hours, and when people come to my gigs, I want them to forget everything about their own life and just be wrapped up in what's going on."

let me ENTER

He also loves working with other stars, and at the 1998 Brits did a 'Full Monty' medley with pop veteran Tom Jones. "That boy has so much energy," said hip-wriggling old-timer Jones, "he makes me feel young again. I think he's one of the most talented and natural performers in Britain today!"

TAIN you

Ego a Go Go

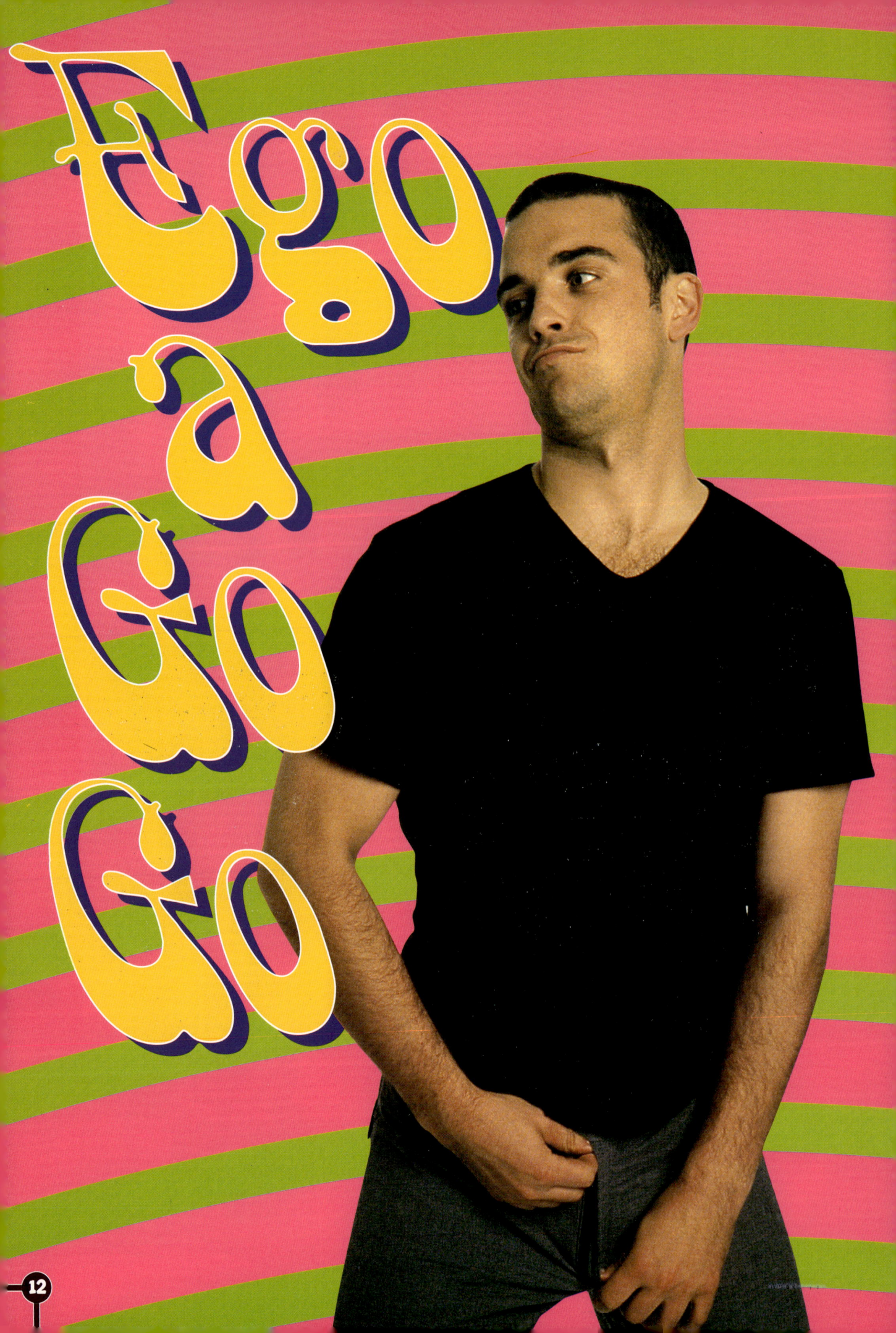

Robbie's a notorious prankster, and likes nothing better than to play the fool. He had a brilliant time making the video for 'Let Me Entertain You'. He got to dress up like weirdy rock band Kiss - complete with black and white face make-up and a skin-tight leather top!

Even when he's not on stage he likes to dress in outrageous costumes. After a gig in Aberdeen, Robbie got kitted out in an Afro-style wig, sunglasses, and a black bin-liner, and handed out cubes of marzipan carved with the initials RW to journalists camped outside his hotel. "It's Robbie's karaoke outfit," said one of his mates. "He's just having a laugh."

she's the one

Robbie's love life has always been a bit rocky. During his Take That days he claims that he was the only one who never had a girlfriend, but all that changed after he left the band. He's had top snogs with the likes of Anna Friel (of Brookside fame), Sporty Spice, a posh sounding make-up girl and (according to the newspapers) plenty of 'mystery blondes'.

"I've had loads of girlfriends and I have been a bit of a tart in my time," admits Robbie sheepishly.

He even got engaged to All Saint Nicole Appleton, splitting up just before Robbie wiped the floor at the 1999 Brit Awards.

But Robbie doesn't have plans to settle down just yet. "I think family comes when you're immensely happy and secure. I'm very happy and secure at the moment. Immensely is the next stage up. I still have so much to work for. I work damn hard. I'm the hardest working man in pop!"

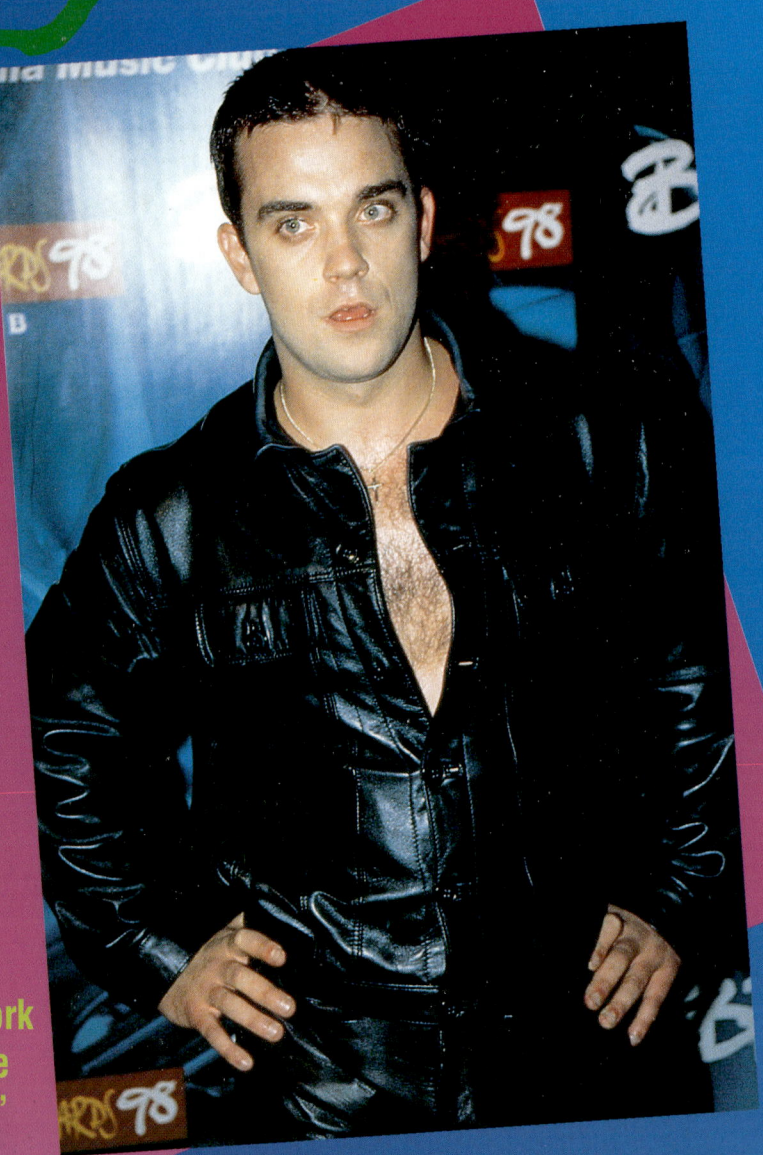

15

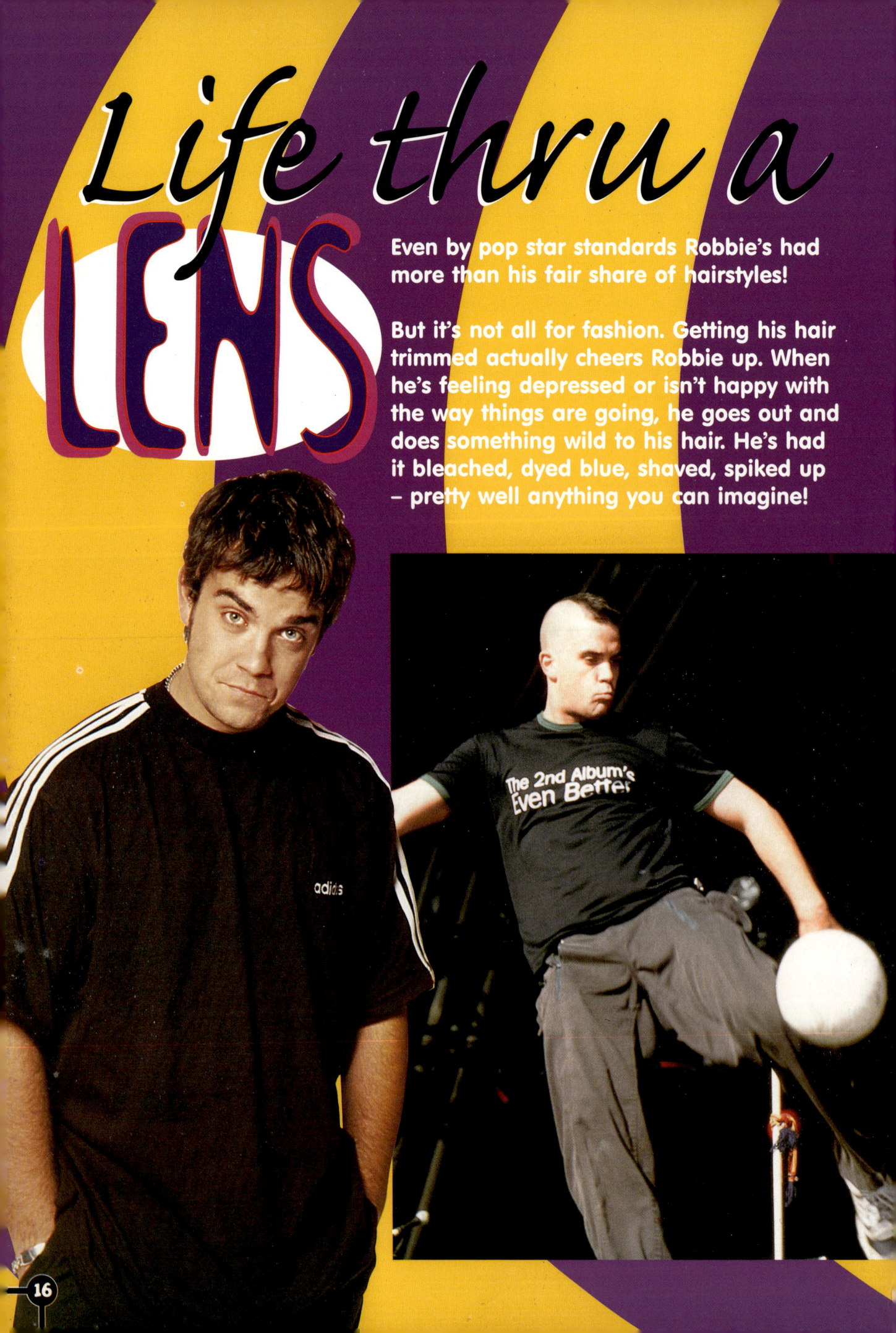

Life thru a LENS

Even by pop star standards Robbie's had more than his fair share of hairstyles!

But it's not all for fashion. Getting his hair trimmed actually cheers Robbie up. When he's feeling depressed or isn't happy with the way things are going, he goes out and does something wild to his hair. He's had it bleached, dyed blue, shaved, spiked up – pretty well anything you can imagine!

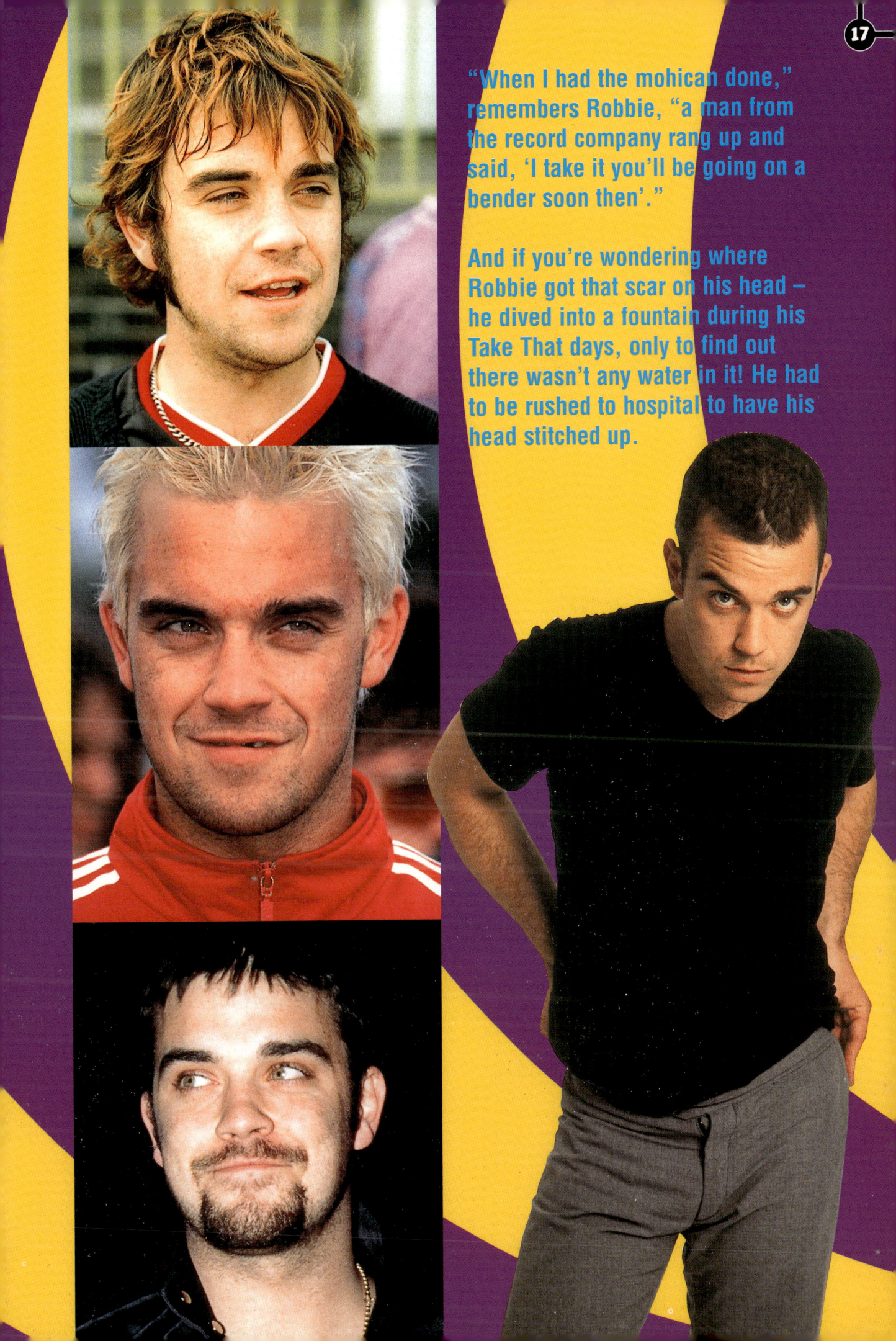

"When I had the mohican done," remembers Robbie, "a man from the record company rang up and said, 'I take it you'll be going on a bender soon then'."

And if you're wondering where Robbie got that scar on his head – he dived into a fountain during his Take That days, only to find out there wasn't any water in it! He had to be rushed to hospital to have his head stitched up.

Man MACHINE

With the release of his first album Robbie shocked fans by proving just how good he was at song-writing! Nobody expected him to be able to write tunes as well as he could sing them, and with top single 'Angels' Robbie showed he had what it takes to be the next Elton John!

He works closely with writing buddy Guy Chambers – a partnership that only came about by chance.

"Guy's name was handed to me on a bit of paper," says Robbie. "I hadn't written anything good for ages so I had this list of writers sent over by the record company and I went '...eerrr him'. Good job I got it right."

Robbie writes his songs really quickly. His first solo album 'Life Thru a Lens' was knocked out in only seven days! "At the time I didn't know if that was a good thing or a bad thing because when you're doing exams and you finish half an hour before the end, you're going to get a 'D'! Most of the songs I've written take two hours, or even an hour to write."

"Ideas are usually just a big mish-mash in my head with choruses and things. I write most of them down but some I just remember. I've got a great memory for lyrics and melodies which is useful considering the game I'm in."

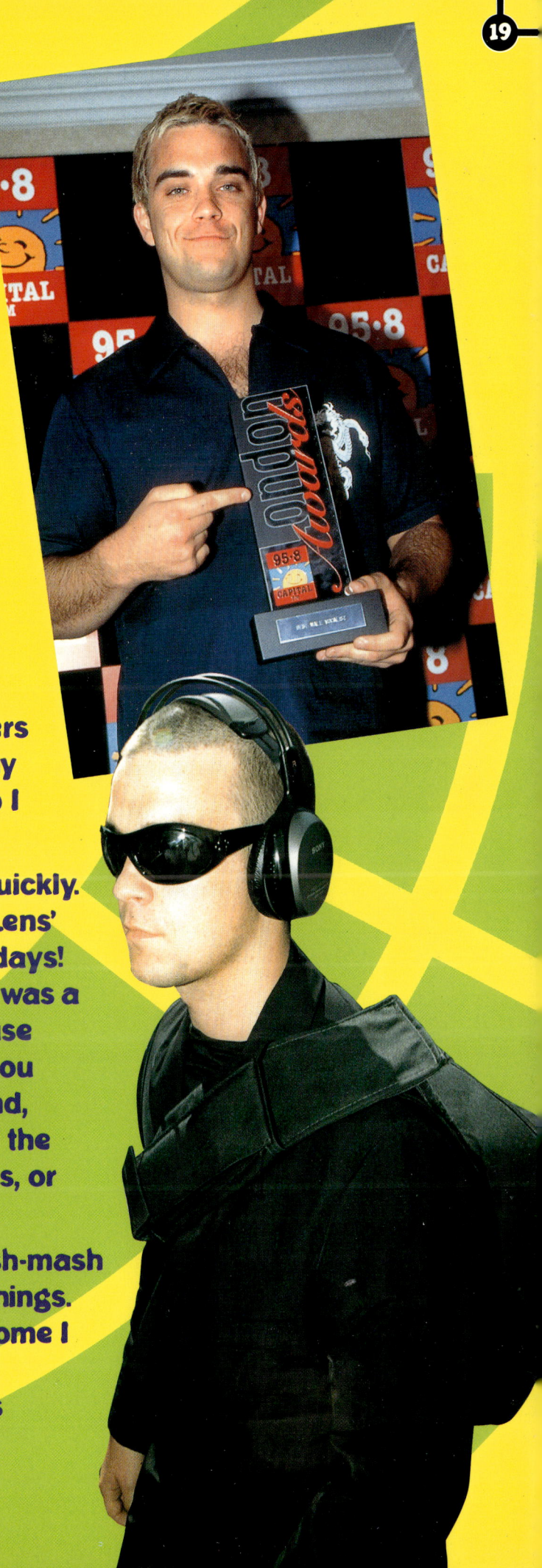

Robbie's got loads of pals from the world of showbiz, including famous musicians, supermodels, top comedians and TV presenters.

But soon, we might be seeing Robbie hanging out with friends from the movie business, because he's hinted that he plans to get into films.

"I'm sure that one day I'll be in a big movie, but at the moment I'm really into my music. I know there are still a lot of surprises ahead in the future for me. That's what makes life so exciting."

HEAVEN F

"I'm going to enjoy every day and whatever's thrown at me."

ROM HERE

One of God's Better People

If there's one person that's really important in Robbie's life, it's his Mum. She's seen him through the hard times and is always there for him when he gets depressed. He wrote the song One Of God's Better People just for her. "I wrote that ballad for my mum," he said proudly. "When I played her the song on my guitar for the first time we were both crying."

Robbie's also dead generous, and loves splashing out on presents. He's bought some great gifts for his Mum, including an original painting by American artist Andy Warhol. It's a portrait of actress Grace Kelly, which he bought off novelist Jeffrey Archer for a whopping £20,000!

23

WIN SOME LOSE SOME

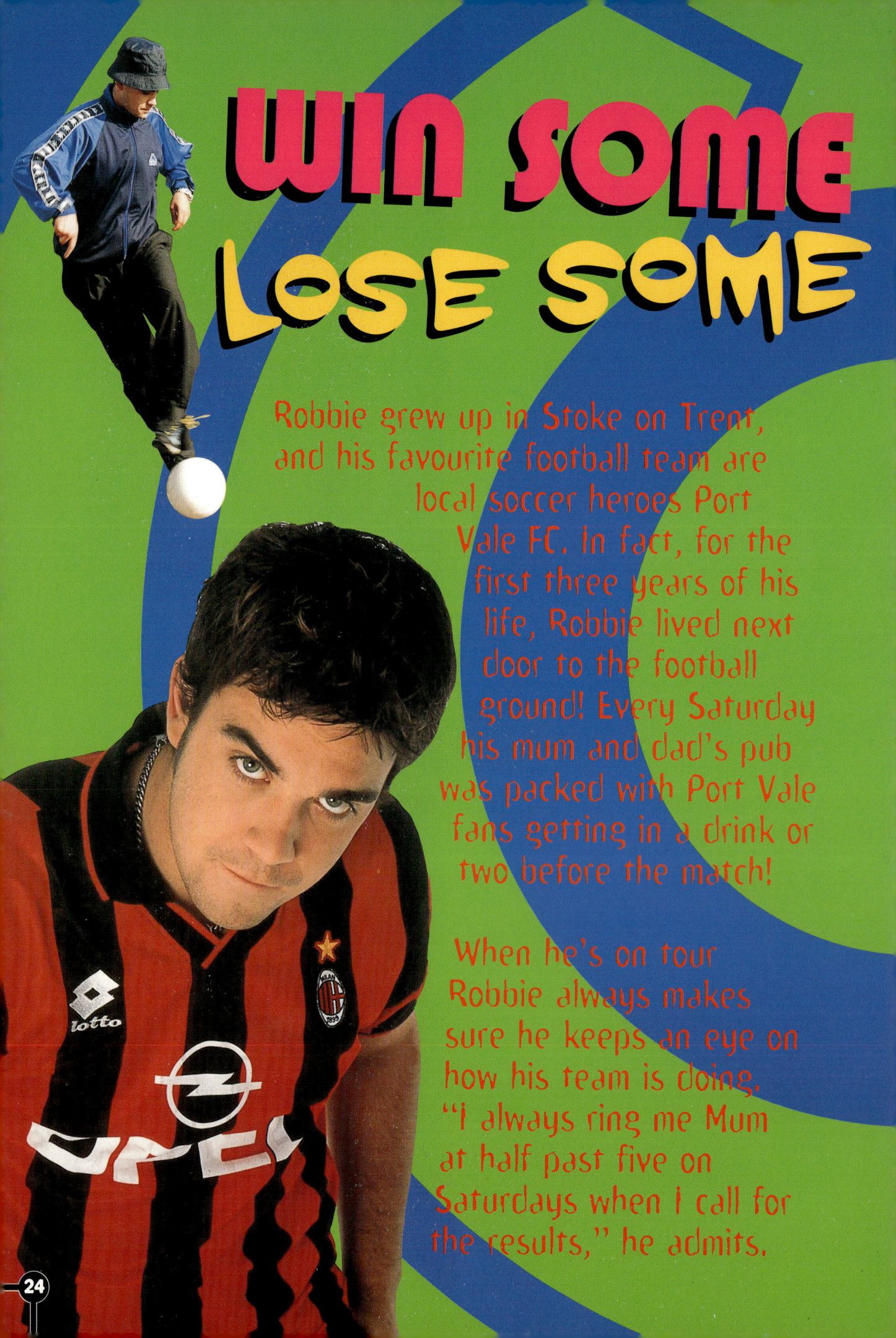

Robbie grew up in Stoke on Trent, and his favourite football team are local soccer heroes Port Vale FC. In fact, for the first three years of his life, Robbie lived next door to the football ground! Every Saturday his mum and dad's pub was packed with Port Vale fans getting in a drink or two before the match!

When he's on tour Robbie always makes sure he keeps an eye on how his team is doing. "I always ring me Mum at half past five on Saturdays when I call for the results," he admits.

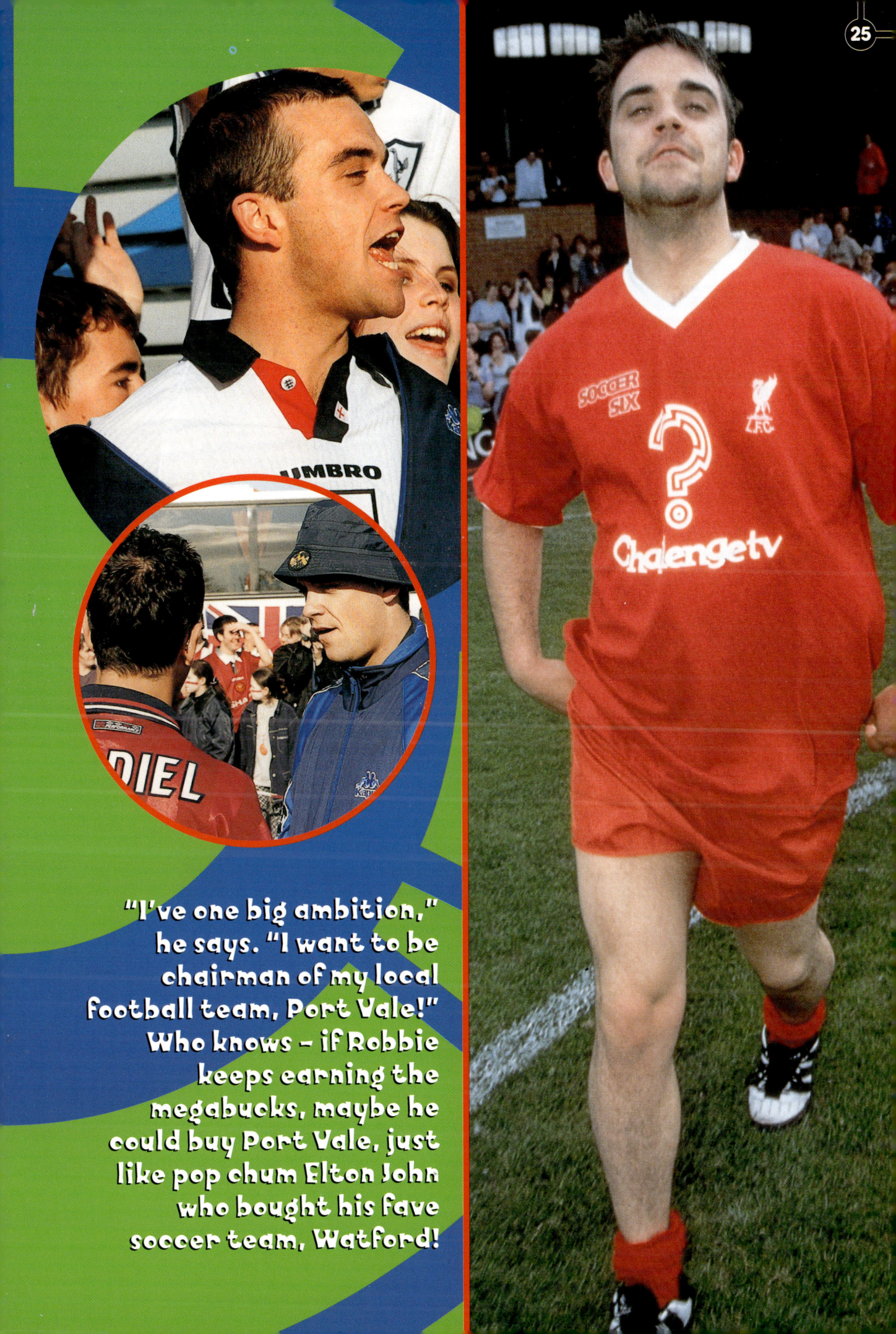

"I've one big ambition," he says. "I want to be chairman of my local football team, Port Vale!" Who knows - if Robbie keeps earning the megabucks, maybe he could buy Port Vale, just like pop chum Elton John who bought his fave soccer team, Watford!

"I have an awful lot of respect for George Michael and **Freedom** is a great song but I left Take That saying I want to be me, I want to do my own songs. And then, amazingly for my first record, I contradicted myself.

Angels was the first record that brought me any satisfaction as a solo artist. **Old Before I Die** was a good little hit but it was **Angels** when I went 'yeah it is dead good innit'."

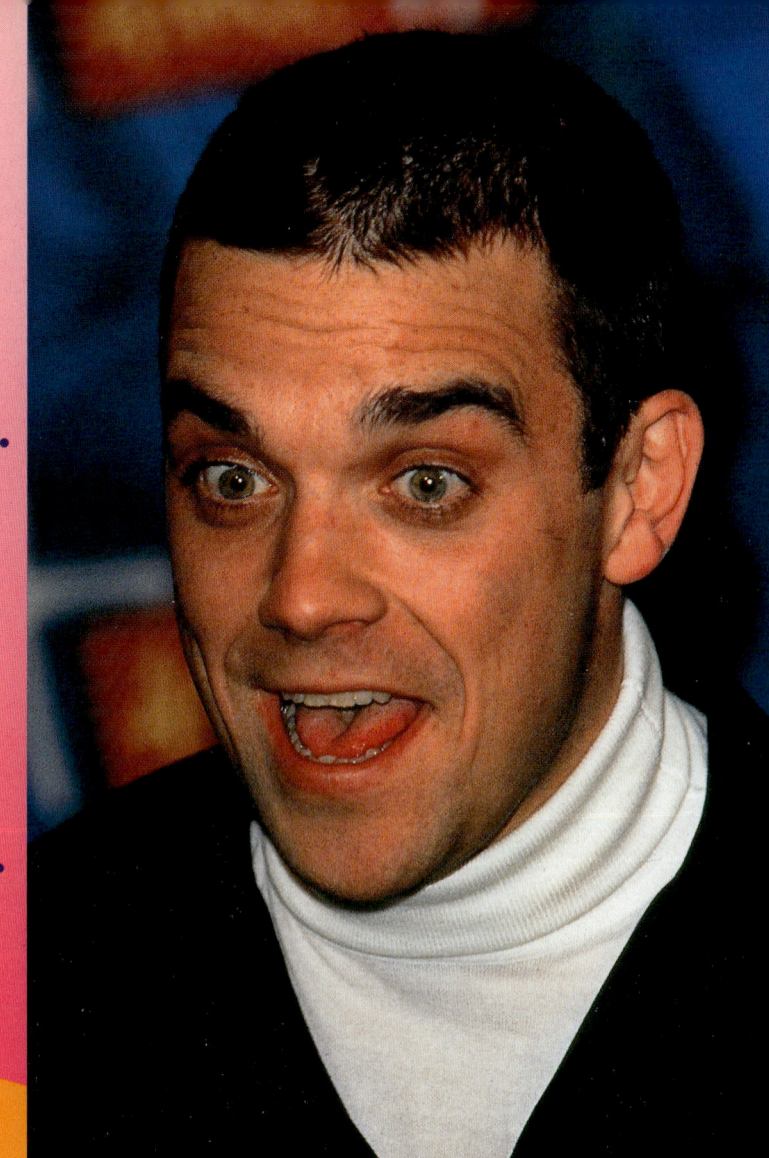

millennium man

"People tell me I can do this for 30 years if I want it and I do think that's the case. If you sing good songs, perform well, keep some character and have charisma then your fan base shouldn't go away."

"I get a real buzz out of being on stage and having all those girls screaming and shouting and throwing their knickers at me."

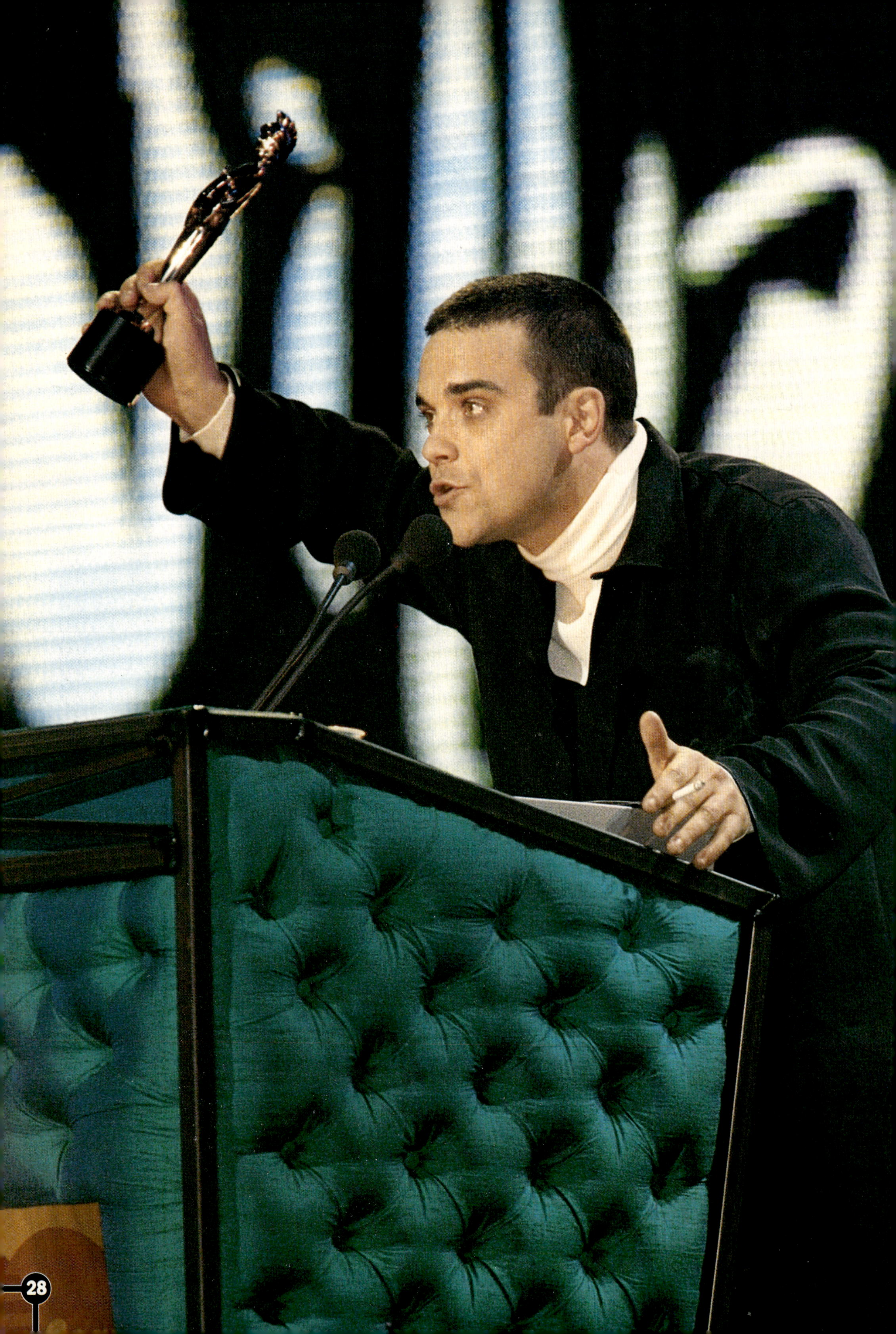

the Brits

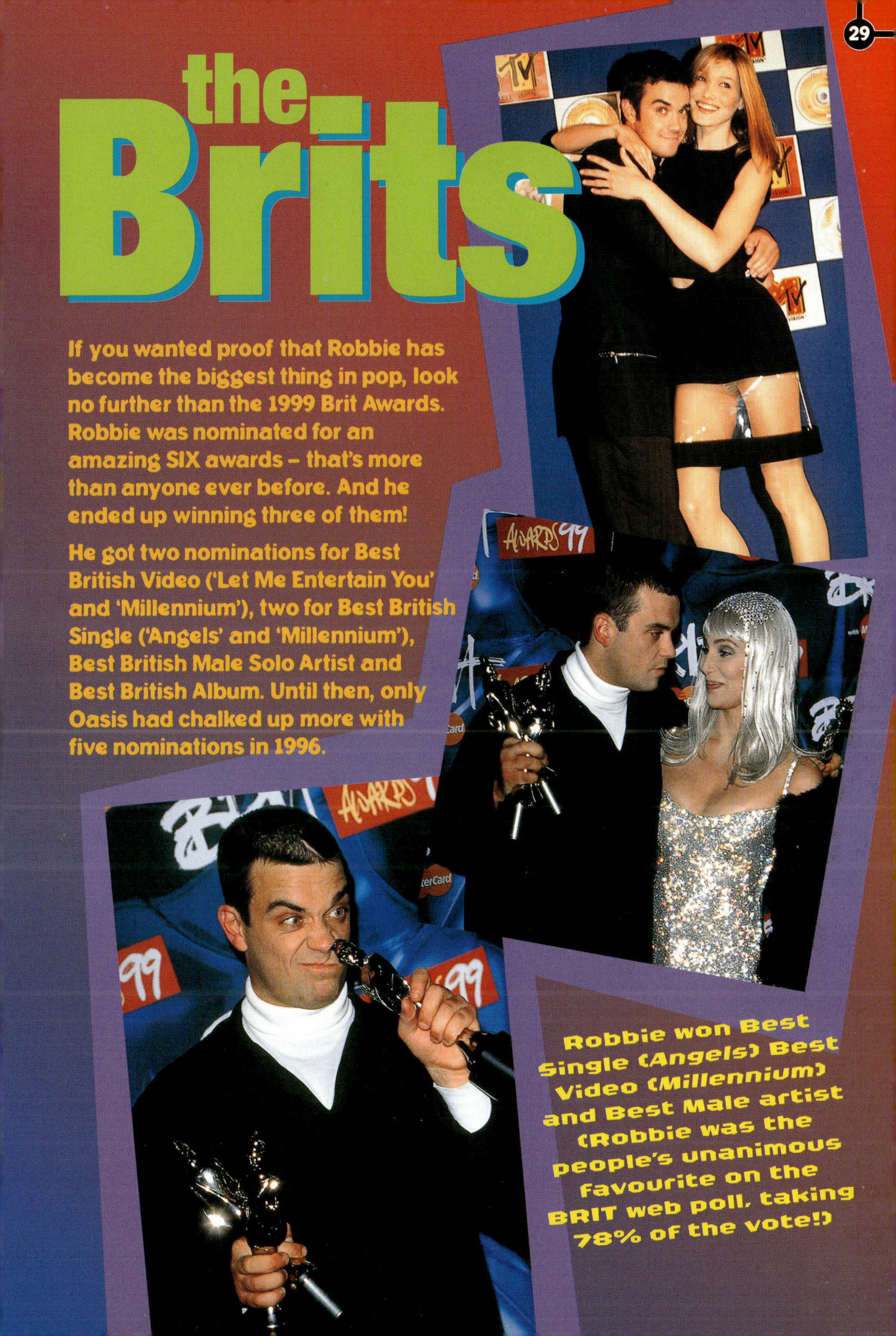

If you wanted proof that Robbie has become the biggest thing in pop, look no further than the 1999 Brit Awards. Robbie was nominated for an amazing SIX awards – that's more than anyone ever before. And he ended up winning three of them!

He got two nominations for Best British Video ('Let Me Entertain You' and 'Millennium'), two for Best British Single ('Angels' and 'Millennium'), Best British Male Solo Artist and Best British Album. Until then, only Oasis had chalked up more with five nominations in 1996.

Robbie won Best Single (Angels) Best Video (Millennium) and Best Male artist (Robbie was the people's unanimous favourite on the BRIT web poll, taking 78% of the vote!)

th
dre

What next for the king of pop?

Robbie plans to get another album out soon.

"I wanted to rattle three off in my first couple of years," he said.

"Not a bad start, heh?"

ese ams

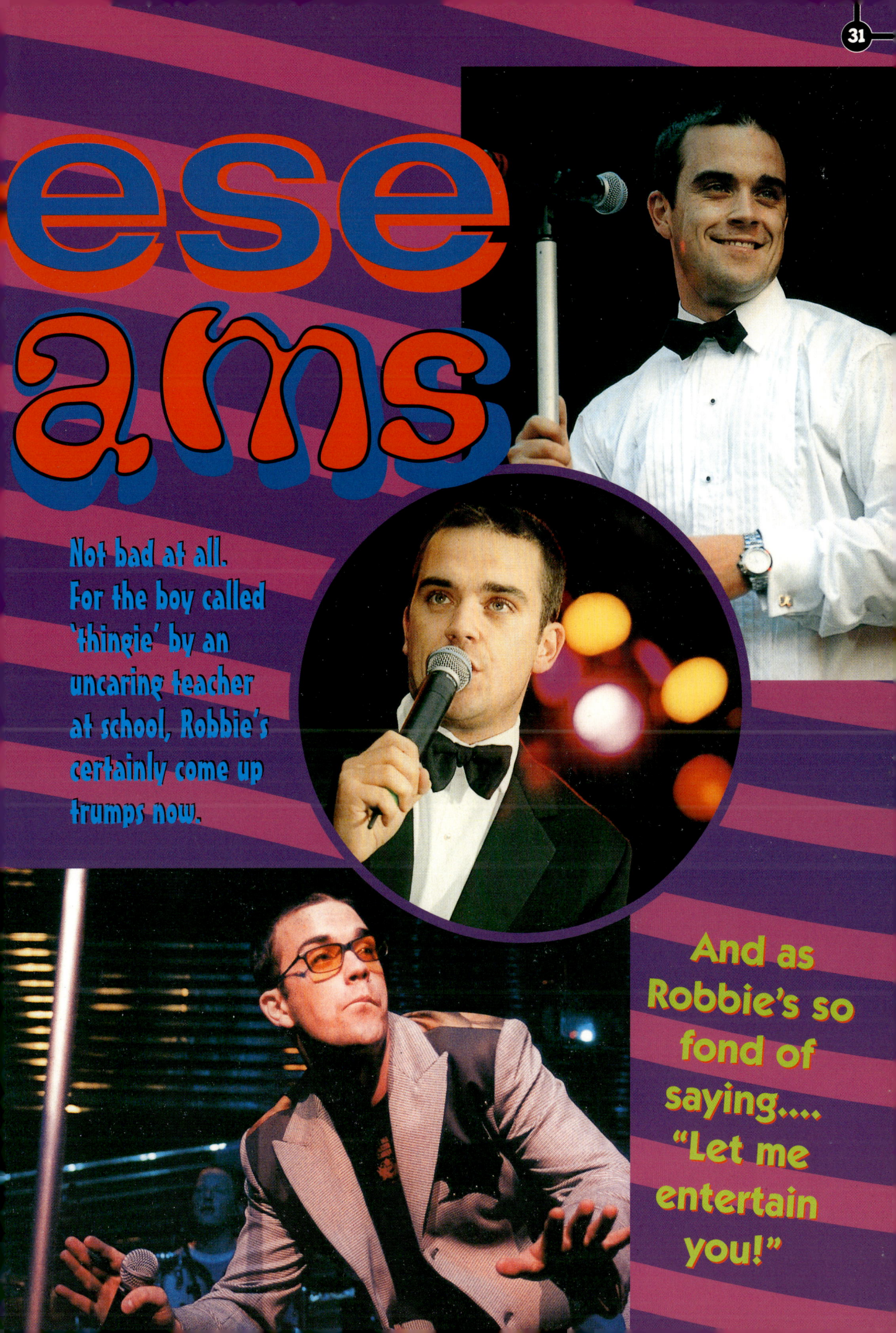

Not bad at all. For the boy called 'thingie' by an uncaring teacher at school, Robbie's certainly come up trumps now.

And as Robbie's so fond of saying.... "Let me entertain you!"

32

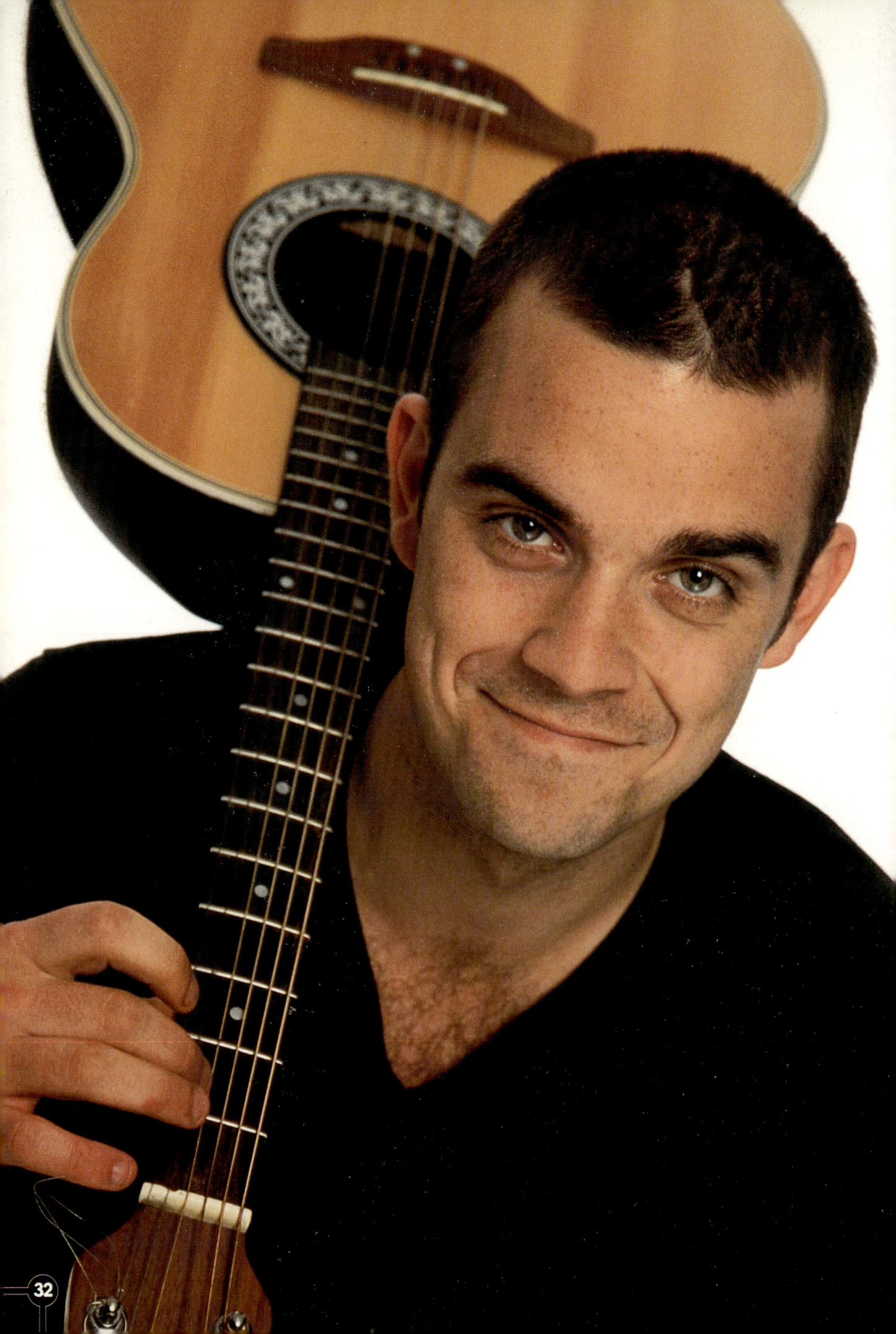